Getting Your Money's Worth

Making Smart Financial Choices

By Diane Dakers

Educational Consultant:
Christopher A. Fons, M.A.
Social Studies and Economics Faculty
Milwaukee Public Schools

 Crabtree Publishing Company
www.crabtreebooks.com

Financial Literacy for Life

Author: Diane Dakers

Series research and development: Reagan Miller

Project coordinator: Mark Sachner, Water Buffalo Books

Editorial director: Kathy Middleton

Editors: Mark Sachner, Janine Deschenes

Proofreader: Wendy Scavuzzo

Photo research: Westgraphix/Tammy West

Designer: Westgraphix/Tammy West

Production coordinator and prepress technician:
Tammy McGarr

Print coordinator: Margaret Amy Salter

Contributing writer and editor: Christopher A. Fons, economics teacher, Riverside University High School, Milwaukee Public Schools

Photographs:
Front cover: All images from Shutterstock

Interior:
Public domain: p. 39.
Shutterstock: pp. 1, 3, 4, 5, 6, 7, 8, 9, 10, 11, 12, 13 (top left, bottom right, and bottom center), 15, 16, 18, 19 (top), 20, 22 (top and middle), 23 (top left, bottom left, bottom right, and background), 24, 25, 26, 27, 31 (top right and bottom left), 32, 34, 36 (bottom left: all; bottom right: center and top), 37, 38, 40, 41, 42, 43 (bottom left and bottom right); Allen.G: p. 13 (far right); Belish: p. 36 (bottom right: right); Billion Photos: p. 31 (top background); Bloomicon: p. 22 (bottom); emka74: p. 43 (far right, bottom); lev radin: p. 36 (bottom right: left); MAHATHIR MOHD YASIN: p. 31 (top left); vvoe: p. 43 (far right, top).
Water Buffalo Books: pp. 19 (bottom), 23 (top right), 33.

Written and produced for Crabtree Publishing Company by Water Buffalo Books

---

Library and Archives Canada Cataloguing in Publication

Dakers, Diane, author
　　　Getting your money's worth : making smart financial choices / Diane Dakers.

(Financial literacy for life)
Includes index.
Issued in print and electronic formats.
ISBN 978-0-7787-3097-2 (hardcover).--
ISBN 978-0-7787-3106-1 (softcover).--ISBN 978-1-4271-1876-9 (HTML)

　　　1. Finance, Personal--Juvenile literature. 2. Saving and investment--Juvenile literature. 3. Shopping--Juvenile literature. 4. Consumer credit--Juvenile literature. 5. Cash transactions--Juvenile literature.
6. Credit ratings--Juvenile literature. 7. Cost and standard of living--Juvenile literature. I. Title.

HG179.D343 2017　　　　j332.024　　　　C2016-907141-3
　　　　　　　　　　　　　　　　　　　　　　　　　C2016-907142-1

Library of Congress Cataloging-in-Publication Data

CIP available at the Library of Congress

Crabtree Publishing Company

www.crabtreebooks.com　　　1-800-387-7650

Printed in Canada/062017/MA20170420

Published in Canada
Crabtree Publishing
616 Welland Ave.
St. Catharines, Ontario
L2M 5V6

Published in the United States
Crabtree Publishing
PMB 59051
350 Fifth Avenue, 59th Floor
New York, New York 10118

Published in the United Kingdom
Crabtree Publishing
Maritime House
Basin Road North, Hove
BN41 1WR

Published in Australia
Crabtree Publishing
3 Charles Street
Coburg North
VIC 3058

Contents

CHAPTER ONE

SPEND TODAY, OR SAVE FOR TOMORROW?

Is your money "burning a hole in your pocket"? Do you want to spend it but feel as though you should save it, too? Knowing when to spend and how to save is an important part of having money. Money is a necessary part of life. We use it to pay for almost everything we need and want, from what we wear to where we live. Most people do not have an endless supply of money. That's why being money wise is essential.

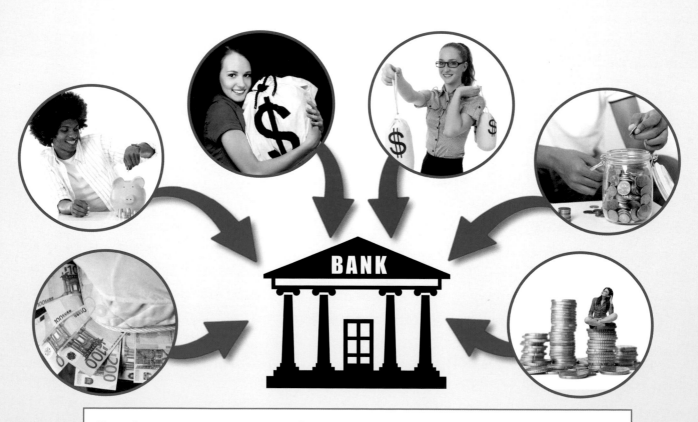

How do you manage your cash? Keeping it in one place until you need to spend it may be one way of managing money. As you get older, however, you will have more money and more things to do with it. Opening a bank account is one of the first things you can do to keep track of exactly how much you are saving and how much you have on hand to spend.

In The "Red" and In The "Black"

There's an old **bookkeeping** term for not having enough money to pay for things. It's called being "in the red." It comes from the practice of recording debt in red ink in accounting books. Black ink was used to record when more money came in than was spent. In terms of your personal spending, being "in the black" is something that requires some knowledge and planning.

Learning the value of money

Thousands of years ago, before money existed, people traded or **bartered** for the things they wanted. A farmer might trade cattle for cloth. If you have ever swapped something you own for something a friend owns, you understand bartering. It is a great system, except for when the value of what one person has to barter does not match the value of what another has to trade.

That's where money comes in handy. Money is a symbol of value. It is something we exchange to buy things. The expression, and title of this book, "getting your money's worth" refers to getting good value for something you paid for. How do you know what is good value or that you have used your money wisely? Knowing how money works can help you understand how to spend it and save it in smart ways.

As you grow older, you'll have household expenses to manage, big purchases to make, such as a new home, and of course you'll want to take well-deserved vacations from time to time! You will quickly learn that money can be difficult to juggle. With careful planning, however, it's possible to have a positive relationship with money and reduce the stress of managing your finances.

Shift

$PEAKING OF MONEY ...

"It doesn't matter how old or young you are, learning how to save and manage your money is vitally important. By starting good financial practices in your youth, you are more likely to maintain these good habits in your adulthood."

U.S. Mint's H.I.P. Pocket Change Web Site

Firm Up Your Financial Smarts

Rather than going through life worrying, feeling guilty, and experiencing jealousy, you can choose to have a healthier relationship with your dollars and cents. You can choose to sharpen your money smarts. This area of expertise is called financial literacy, and it's something you can start working on right now.

Learn the Language of Money

Financial literacy is about learning the language of money and becoming comfortable speaking that language. It's about understanding how to earn money, keep track of it, and save and spend it wisely. Mostly, financial literacy is about learning how money works and how it can work for you.

Many people consider money a **taboo** subject or something that is not acceptable to talk about in public. Not talking about money, though, is one of the things that can lead to financial problems in life.

Earning money, keeping track of it, spending and saving wisely. These are some of the important ingredients leading to financial literacy and success.

BE CAREFUL OUT THERE

HUSH MONEY

Because there are so many people ready to separate you from your money, it's important not to discuss your dollars with just anyone. Of course, you should talk about *everything* related to your finances with your parents or guardians. Otherwise, think before you speak.

When you're out shopping, for example, it's *not* a good idea to discuss out loud how much cash you're carrying in your purse or pocket. You never know who might be listening.

The same is true of money in a bank account and your family's financial **status**. If the wrong people find out that you, or your family, have a lot of money stashed away, they may try to cheat, steal, or otherwise take it from you.

Most people you will meet in life will be trustworthy, kind, and honest, but money can influence some people to act differently. Greed can lead certain people to do mean, unethical, and dishonest things.

That doesn't mean you can't trust anyone when it comes to your money. It is, however, important to be aware that greedy people exist, and to be cautious when it comes to sharing your personal money matters.

To Save or Not to Save—That Is the Question

Do you have a piggy bank, bank account, or other stash of money? Is it full of coins? Or do you empty it every time you want to buy something? This question of whether to save or spend is one you will be asking yourself for your whole life. As you grow up, the **stakes**–and the number of demands on your hard-earned dollars–will get higher and higher.

It's important to learn how to save and spend wisely today, before your finances get complicated tomorrow.

Right now, you might earn an allowance. You may earn that money by doing chores around the house, or even doing work for your family's business, such as a farm or a store. You might get a few bucks on your birthday and other occasions, too. Maybe you mow people's lawns or shovel their sidewalks for extra pocket money.

If you're like many people, the first thing you want to do when cash comes your way is spend it right away on the things you want. As you grow older, and your responsibilities become more "grown-up," you may find that you have to spend money almost as soon as you get it–but on things you need, not just want. Buying food and clothing, and paying monthly bills for rent, heat, electricity, phone, and even internet service, will all make urgent demands on your wallet and savings.

Socking It Away

Spending money is one of the easiest things to do in life. There are plenty of people, stores, and businesses out there just waiting to separate you from your money. There are also endless numbers of wonderful things tempting you to buy them—books, games, makeup, junk food, jewelry, movie tickets, and everything else your heart desires.

What if the thing your heart desires is something expensive—such as a flashy electronic gadget or deluxe skateboard?

You're going to have to save up some of your earnings. It might take you a few weeks or months of saving, for example, to raise the cash to buy the board or electronic gadget of your dreams.

This is where financial literacy skills come in. By learning when (and how much) to save, how to spend wisely, and ways to manage your moolah in the long term, you'll be making the most of your money in no time.

Figuring out how much money to put in your piggy bank and how much to take out may seem like **child's play**. But it's a useful early step on the path to managing your money as you grow older and your expenses become greater and more complicated.

A PENNY SAVED IS A PENNY EARNED

You might not have a whole lot of money right now, but you're not too young to start developing healthy financial habits. As soon as money starts coming your way, that's the time to start figuring out what to do with it. What you might *want* to do with your dollars is spend, spend, spend! What you might think you *should* do with your money is save it all. The truth is that you can do both. You can spend, save, or even give it away if you feel like it. The important thing is to make educated choices. If you start smart, you'll be money savvy for life.

You're never too young to begin figuring out how you want to manage your own money!

?

WEIGHING THE COST WHEN YOU CASH THAT PAYCHECK

Katari has started a part-time job at a local grocery store and received his first paycheck. He wanted to cash his **check**, but he didn't have a bank account. So he went to a "Check and Go" check-cashing service. Check and Go charges him a fee of $10 to cash his check. If Katari cashes his paychecks each week at Check and Go, he will have spent $40 a month in check-cashing fees.

Katari is thinking about opening a no-cost bank account to deposit his checks into. Opening this account will save him $480 a year in check-cashing fees. But using cash helps Katari easily track how much money he has to spend. Having the account would mean that he must now keep track of the balance, or amount of money, in his account to avoid taking out more than he has deposited. If he **overdraws**, or takes out more money than is in his account, he will have to pay a fine. On top of that, some bank accounts are no-cost only if the balance is kept above a minimum total dollar amount.

What would you do?

Making Plans

When you get your weekly allowance or a bit of birthday money—or a paycheck for working part-time at a drug store—your first **impulse** might be to go out and buy that new video game you've had your eye on. But, if you blow every buck that comes your way, how will you ever save up enough for the remote-controlled drone you also have your eye on?

The answer is to spend some and save some. A smart approach is to divide the money you have left over after paying bills into three chunks as soon as it comes in:

1. Pay yourself first.

Financial experts suggest setting aside 10 **percent** of all your **income** in a "rainy day," or emergency, account. The idea is to leave this money untouched, and regularly add to it. That way, you will have cash-on-hand for unexpected needs. For example, you might accidentally break your grandmother's favorite lamp, and your parents say you have to pay to replace it.

Pay myself.

Save to meet my goals.

Have some fun!

2. Save to meet your goals.

Into the second pot of money goes the cash you save to meet your longer-term financial goals—buying that skateboard, for example, or possibly for some more expensive goals, such as a computer. (Some kids even start thinking about the day when they will be more financially independent later in their teenage years, which means they might start saving early for a car, or to go to college.) Watch this fund grow until you've saved enough to fulfill your goals!

3. Have some fun.

After the first two chunks of money are set aside, what's left is your spending money, or "fun money"—cash to spend day to day.

Congratulations

EDUCATION PROGRAMS

EDUCATION PROGRAMS

EDUCATION PROGRAMS

EDUCATION PROGRAMS

EDUCATION PROGRAMS

EDUCATION PROGRAMS

EDUCATION PROGRAMS

How Much Cash Should You Stash?

Deciding how much money to save and how much to spend is a bit of a balancing act. You might want to save *all* your money, so you can reach your goals as soon as possible. However, if you save everything, you won't have any left over for day-to-day spending. That isn't realistic, and can result in you scrapping the **budget** altogether!

On the other hand, too much spending money means that your savings will grow very, very slowly.

It takes some thought and practice to balance your spending and saving. Once you have a plan that works for you, you'll be able to see your "rainy, day" fund grow and to meet your short- and long-term goals. And, you'll have a realistic amount of spending money along the way. Most importantly, you'll be setting yourself up for lifelong financial success!

FOCUS ON FINANCE — Planning for Tomorrow

It's important to decide on spending and saving goals as a part of a smart financial **strategy**.

Short-term financial goals are things you can achieve with the cash you have on hand. For you, a short-term goal might be to buy a new leash for your dog, go out for a snack with your friends, or spend an hour in an arcade.

Medium-term financial goals require a small to medium amount of saving. This could be a few weeks' allowance. Goals in this category might include such things as purchasing a pair of shoes, planning the perfect Halloween costume, or buying new earbuds.

Long-term financial goals take time to reach. These are expensive items or activities that require weeks or months of saving—a digital camera, rock-climbing lessons, or a new bicycle, for example.

Your goals will become even longer-term as you grow up. These might include saving for a new car, a college education, or a house. Sooner than you think, you'll even have to start saving for retirement.

You may not need to start thinking about life-changing goals like these just yet, but the more you learn about financial literacy now, the more able you'll be in the future to meet your long-long-long-term goals.

Savvy Saving

Once you've decided to sock away some savings, you have a few choices about where to stash that cash. Hiding it under your mattress is not the best idea. A better plan is to deposit it in a savings account at a bank or credit union. Both types of **financial institutions** are safe places to keep your money. They offer similar services—but they have a few important differences.

Banks and Credit Unions— Similar but Different

Banks are businesses designed to make money. They are usually large **corporations** with **branches** in many cities and countries. Usually, any adult can open a bank account at a bank.

Credit unions, on the other hand, are **not-for-profit (or nonprofit) organizations**. They are actually owned by their members. These are the customers who do their banking there.

A bank (or credit union) offers many services that will be useful as you become more financially savvy. As a "home base" for your money, a bank is a great place to keep your cash safe. It can also be a place where you set aside "rainy day" money for emergencies. As you grow older, you'll find that it also offers lots of other things. These include **credit cards**, loans for homes and cars, financial planning services, and advice for putting your money in plans where it can grow in value.

All the money a credit union makes goes back into the organization, or into the pockets of its members. Credit unions are usually community-based with few branches. Members usually have something in common that qualifies them for membership. They may live in the same area. They may work in the same industry or field (teaching, for example, or factory work such as beer brewing or car manufacturing). They may have family members who belong to a credit union, or belong to the same interest group (church members or graduates of a particular university). Credit unions usually offer financial services that appeal to members of these groups.

Because of their business structure, credit unions often have lower (and fewer) service fees than banks do. However, because they are smaller organizations, credit unions might also offer fewer online or financial services, and their branches and cash machines, or ATMs (Automated, or Automatic, Teller Machines), may be harder to find.

Some Interesting Things About Interest

Most people put money into the bank for safe-keeping, to **withdraw** and spend at a later time. The money you deposit in your account is pooled with the money every other customer in the bank deposits. The bank loans this money out to other individuals or businesses, or **invests** it. People who receive a bank loan pay the bank a fee called **interest** for borrowing money from the bank. This is one way banks earn **profits**. In other words, the bank itself borrows the money in its customers' accounts to make more money. The bank then pays part of that profit to you—the customer—as a monthly fee, also called interest, for the privilege of borrowing the money in your account.

The percentage rates at which banks lend and borrow money make up a large part of the business of banking.

Interest rates paid to customers at banks and credit unions change regularly but are usually quite low. In 2016, *Business Insider* magazine reported that current interest rates were "at the lowest levels in the last 5,000 years of civilization." That means you won't earn much interest on the money you put in the bank or credit union. Even with such low interest rates, however, banks and credit unions are the most **secure** places to keep your money.

Banks and credit unions each have pros and cons. The bottom line is to ask many questions before you deposit your dough into any financial institution—and definitely discuss it with your parents, guardians, and other trusted adults.

The Business of Banking

Most banks and credit unions offer a variety of types of accounts. The main ones you need to know about right now are savings and checking accounts.

Both types of accounts earn interest every month, but savings accounts generally offer slightly higher interest rates than checking accounts. In recent years, the difference has usually been tiny because interest rates are so low.

That is one difference between checking and savings accounts. The biggest difference between them is, as the name suggests, that checking accounts allow you to write checks.

Because of the increased use of **debit cards**, ATMs, and **online banking**, checks are used less and less around the world today. Many financial institutions in Europe, for example, no longer offer customers checks at all. In North America, the use of checks is also on the decline, but checking accounts are still available.

BE CAREFUL OUT THERE

HOW SAFE IS SAFE?

Depositing money at a bank or credit union is the safest way to store your hard-earned savings. That's because financial institutions have deposit **insurance** that protects customers from losing money if anything goes wrong. In Canada, deposits up to $100,000 are protected. In the United States, deposits of up to $250,000 are insured. That means if the bank goes out of business, you will get your money back—up to these amounts.

Banks also have extra insurance to cover bank robberies. Either way, your money is protected—certainly more so than it would be if it were hidden under your mattress!

F⊙CUS ON FINANCE

Saving for the Long, Long, Long Term

Believe it or not, retirement is something that should be on your radar as soon as you start earning a regular income.

In Canada and the United States, people save for retirement by putting money into retirement savings plans. Many employers also make monthly contributions to retirement plans on behalf of their employee**s**.

Whether you organize a private plan, or take part in a retirement program through your workplace, it's a good idea to contribute to it through **automatic payments**. These payments are electronically taken out of your paycheck, bank, or credit union account and deposited in your retirement plan. That way, your money is set aside before you even see it, and you won't even notice it's gone!

Retirement is a long, long way off for you. It might be 10 years before you even get your first full-time job. When you get that job, though, you'll know what to do to secure your future. Set up a retirement fund, deposit money every month, and watch it grow!

Time to Take It Out

The whole point of depositing your dollars in a bank account is to meet your medium- and long-term financial goals. (Remember to look into maintaining a separate account for your "rainy day," or emergency, fund.)

When you've saved enough money to meet one of your financial goals—buying that drone, for example—it's time to reward yourself for planning ahead, managing your money, and having the self-discipline to save. It's time to take back your bucks!

Of course, you can only take out the amount of money you've put into your account, along with any added interest.

How It Works

To take cash out of your account, you simply go to a branch of your bank or credit union and withdraw it. If you have ATM privileges, you could also take out money at a bank machine. (There are usually limits to how much you can withdraw from an ATM in a 24-hour period.)

ATMs provide bank customers with quick and easy access to their accounts. With great convenience, however, comes great responsibility. It's up to you to be sure you have enough money in your account!

BE CAREFUL OUT THERE

IT PAYS TO ASK

Before you open an account at a bank or credit union, you should do some research—even if you choose to use the same institution your parents use. Here are some sample questions:

1. Where is the nearest branch?
2. What are the different types of accounts available? Are there accounts specifically designed for young people, or accounts that could be used for a "rainy day" fund?
3. At what interest rates do the different accounts earn money?
4. What personal information, identification, or other paperwork, is required to open an account?
5. Is there a minimum amount I must deposit to open an account?
6. What are the fees associated with the accounts? Must I maintain a **minimum balance** to avoid fees? Is there a fee for every check I write, or for every time I use a debit card?
7. How soon after I deposit money is it available to withdraw? Is there a limit on the number of monthly withdrawals I can make?
8. Where are the ATMs? What are the fees for using an ATM?
9. Is online banking available? Is there a fee for this?

Do not hesitate to ask any question that is important to you before you agree to do business with a financial institution.

ACCOUNT ACCOUNTABILITY

Give It a Try, and DIY

Be **accountable** for your account! When you're ready to open a bank or credit union account, do your research to find what institutions are near your home. Then begin your search for the most suitable financial institution for you. Have an adult on hand for each step of this activity.

Use the list of sample questions in "It Pays to Ask" (p. 20) to give you some ideas, and then make a chart listing the banks and credit unions you're considering. Create a set of columns with the following:

1. **IN COLUMN 1: Write the name of each institution you are considering.**

2. **IN COLUMN 2: Write a question you want answered.**

3. **IN COLUMN 3 AND FOLLOWING COLUMNS: Continue with more questions, one at the top of each column. Include questions you have, as well as the questions trusted adults in your life want to ask.**

Research online to find as many answers as you can for each bank and credit union. Write the answers for each institution.

Highlight the things that are most important to you. For example, low fees might be more important than having a branch around the corner. Ask your parents or guardians to help you with these choices.

Based on the information in your chart, and the **priorities** you've identified, make a **short list** of banks and credit unions that interest you.

With an adult, visit each institution on your short list. Ask questions, look around, and talk to employees. See how friendly and helpful people are. As a kid, you are probably the best person to be able to tell whether grown-ups are taking you seriously! Consult with your parents or guardians to decide which institution is the best choice for you and your money.

Name of Institution	Special accounts for kids?	Interest rate?	Nearest ATM?	Minimum balance?
First National Bank	Yes	1.5 %	0.5 mile	$500
First Savings and Loan	Yes	1.75 %	1 mile	$100
Workers' Credit Union	No	1.0 %	2 blocks	$0

More Ways to Pay

These days, you can also pay *without* cash at most businesses. Most bank accounts include debit cards, which allow you to electronically pay for things with money from your bank account. Some stores accept checks as payment, which you can write if you have a checking account. People also pay with credit cards, and a variety of other methods, including **apps** on your smartphone. There are so many ways to pay for purchases now that spending money is super-easy...and a bit baffling at the same time.

Now that you've learned about how to save your money, it's time to learn how to spend it wisely.

At most businesses, anything you can buy with cash is also available by credit card or debit card. Some also accept checks. Many places are also equipped to handle purchases made by scanning an app on your smartphone.

Bank

Educators
CREDIT UNION

If you save wisely, you'll see your dollars add up!

$ + $ = $$

23

CHAPTER THREE

RETAIL THERAPY

Spending money can be fun. If you're having a bad day, treating yourself to a little trinket can lift your spirits. Who doesn't love getting something shiny and new? Sometimes, though, you might come home from the mall wondering what happened to the pocket full of cash you had when you left home a few hours earlier. Sometimes, doling out dollars is so easy that you don't even realize how many you're handing out. Right now, you're young, and don't have a lot of money to lose. That makes this the perfect time to start practicing healthy spending habits—before any serious splurging tendencies take hold.

Getting out and buying goodies with your friends can be a great bonding experience. For many people, shopping can even be **therapeutic** if you're feeling a little down. However, if you spend a lot of money every time you shop, you'll soon run out. That's why it's important to resist the urge to splurge every time you feel the need to unload some cash!

Think Before You Spend

One of these days, when you check your bank balance, you'll discover you've saved enough money to meet one of your financial goals. First of all, pat yourself on the back—your saving and self-discipline have paid off! Next, take a deep breath before you run to the store to spend that money.

Just because you finally have the cash in hand doesn't mean you should head out to buy the first set of wireless earbuds or new skateboard deck you see. It's all too easy to dash to the nearest store, and plunk down your dollars. You're excited! You've waited, you've saved, and you're ready to buy.

With any purchase—especially big purchases—it's important to make a plan before you hand over your savings. It pays to shop around, search for sales, and weigh your options.

Thanks to the internet, you can research anything before you buy. In fact, you've probably done some surfing while you've been saving.

Look Before You Leap

Before you head to the store, read online reviews to help you decide which skateboard decks, for example, are the best ones for you to consider. Which ones are in your price range? Which ones are available at local stores, so you can check them out in person?

Different stores often sell the same products at different prices, so it's smart to shop around and compare costs. Some stores offer discount coupons. Most have sales sooner or later. Check online, or in your local newspaper for weekly flyers to see where the bargains are.

Browse items online, deposit them in your electronic shopping cart, and pay instantly by credit card. It's as easy as ABC. Before you commit to an online purchase, however, you should check other sites to read reviews and compare prices. By the time you're ready to make your purchase, you'll be an informed shopper.

You'll be amazed at how far your money will go when you start paying attention to how, when, and where you spend it. You might end up waiting a little longer to get the perfect deck at the perfect price, but when you do, you'll feel like you've hit the jackpot!

The important thing is to put on the brakes before you break out the big bucks. But it's not only the large purchases that require some planning.

Decisions, Decisions

By now, if you've been divvying up all your dough into three chunks—an emergency fund, savings to meet financial goals, and your spending money—you'll know exactly how much spending money you can afford to put in your pocket for a trip to the mall.

How you dish out these day-to-day dollars is up to you, but it's always worth planning ahead to get the biggest bang for your limited bucks.

So Many T-Shirts to Consider...

Say you've outgrown your favorite T-shirt, so it's time to buy a new one.

You could go to a trendy **boutique** or specialty shop and buy an expensive new top with the logo of a pricey fashion brand splashed across it. That way, everyone will know you have great taste!

On the other hand, you could choose to shop at the local department store. There, you could buy a plain T-shirt or one with a nice—but not designer—image on it. You'd still have a fine new shirt, and you'd save a lot of money.

Instead of making a trendy, high-end boutique the first stop in your quest for a new article of clothing, you might find something you like, and save a lot of money, in a department store.

Spur-of-the-Moment Spending

Many people put down their money, or hand over their credit cards, without giving it a second thought. What they see is what they buy. They want what they want, and they want it now. This is called **impulse buying**, and it's a dangerous way to spend money. It means paying without planning.

Not all impulse buys are serious cause for concern. In any budget, or financial plan, it's a good idea to allow yourself a bit of fun money. If you feel like blowing a buck or two on a pack of gum at the grocery store checkout, it's not going to ruin you.

Impulse buying becomes dangerous, though, when it's the only kind of shopping you do. It's a sure-fire way to lose track of your money and to pay more for something than you should. People often suffer from "buyer's **remorse**" after an impulse buy. This means that they regret spending their precious dollars on something they later wish they hadn't purchased.

Get Your Priorities in Order

Spending wisely means paying attention to your priorities. In this case, you're the only one who knows which is more important to you—being trendy or saving money. Each choice comes with pros and cons. Smart spending is about weighing the options, and making informed decisions that work for you.

Another thing to consider is the difference between needs and wants.

Buying a new shirt is a *need*. Your other top is too small. You *need* a new one—but do you really need the shirt with the pricey logo? That probably falls in the *want* category. The rule is if you can survive without an item for a reasonable period of time, it's a want, not a *need*.

Even if something isn't a need, it doesn't necessarily mean you shouldn't buy it. It's just one more piece of information to keep in mind as you weigh the pros and cons of a potential purchase.

Pros   Cons   Needs   Wants

SHOPPING SMARTS

Give It a Try, and DIY

Are you a smart shopper? Or a super spender? To understand your buying habits, the first step is to keep track of them. Here's one plan to stay on top of your spending:

1. Create a chart or spreadsheet to track your purchases. It should have at least 5 columns. The first column in your chart should be the date you bought the item. The columns that follow should identify different categories of items you spend money on. Examples include food, clothing, sports, transportation, and entertainment. The final column tracks the reason why you bought the item.

2. For two weeks, record everything you spend money on. Record the date and how much you spent. Write the amount in the column that reflects the category of the purchase. For example, if you spent $7 on lunch with friends, write $7 in the "Food" column.

3. Document why you made each purchase. Was it an impulse buy? Were you hungry? Did you feel peer pressure to purchase? Did you need something, or want it? Be honest about your reasons!

4. At the end of two weeks, review the chart. Add up the amount you spent in each category, and the total amount of money you spent.

Date	Food	Phone	Transportation	Clothes	Why did I buy?
May 15	$3.25				friends insisted I go out for pizza
May 15		$10.00			saw a phone case I liked
May 17	$5.00				had to purchase lunch at school
May 23			$1.25		stayed late and had to take bus
May 27				$80.00	saw new shoes I HAD to have
Subtotals	$8.25	$10.00	$1.25	$80.00	
				Grand Total	$99.50

The Ways One Pays

Once you've decided to buy something, you have another choice to make. How will you pay for it?

A century ago, that choice was easy. Consumers, or customers, had two ways to pay for goods—cash or check. Then came credit cards. And debit cards. And online shopping. And credit-debit cards, prepaid credit cards, and **PayPal**.

Today, you can shop in a store, over the telephone, or on your computer, tablet, or smartphone. You can choose from dozens of different credit cards. You can shop locally, nationally, and internationally. Spending options have exploded—so it's important to understand the ups and downs of each payment method.

Cash and Checks: Old-School, but Still in Style!

Cash is an easy way to pay for something. You open your wallet, pull out some bills and coins, and hand them over. Having cash means going to a bank or ATM before you buy.

Checks are becoming less common today, but some stores still take them. To pay by check, you have to have a checking account. When you're ready to make your purchase, you fill in a check with the name of the business, the date, and the amount of money you are authorizing the store to take from your bank or credit union account. You sign the check, show some identification—to prove you have the right to write the check—and give it to the cashier.

THINK FOR YOURSELF

What Kind of Spender Are You?

Once you've kept track of your purchases and added up some numbers, take a closer look at what you've recorded. See what kinds of conclusions you can reach about your spending habits.

- Ask yourself some questions:
  - Where did you spend most of your money?
  - How much of your spending was spur-of-the-moment? How much was planned?
  - Are there any purchases you wish you hadn't made?
  - What other observations can you make about your spending habits?
- Make note of which purchases you consider "good" purchases, and which could have benefited from more thought.
- Based on your spending, and reasons for spending, what are some ways you could have saved money, or spent it more wisely? How will you apply these ideas in the future?

Debit Cards: Cash on Demand

Debit cards are connected directly to your bank account. You can use a debit card to withdraw cash at an ATM, but you can also use it for **point-of-sale** payment. The point of sale is the place where you pay for something, usually a cashier's counter at a store or business.

When you use your debit card, you swipe it or insert it into a chip-reading machine, then punch in your Personal Identification Number (PIN). This is a secret number that helps ensure no one else is able to use your card. If the payment is approved, money is moved electronically to the store from your account.

The age at which someone is permitted to have a debit card varies by financial institution.

BE CAREFUL OUT THERE

KNOW YOUR BOTTOM LINE

Having a bank or credit union account and a debit card makes it easy to pay for purchases at a store. It's important, though, to keep track of how much money is in your account. You can only spend what you have.

Imagine shopping at your favorite store and choosing the perfect armload of items to purchase. After waiting in line to pay, you reach the cashier—and your debit card is rejected. You can't buy anything. Or you're on your way to the movies with friends. You're out of cash, so you dash to the ATM to refill your wallet. There's no money there, so there's no movie for you.

Some bank accounts will allow you to overdraw, or withdraw more money than you have. There's always a fee for that privilege, though. It's not bad to have this as a safety net for emergencies, but living in your **overdraft** isn't good financial planning.

Running your bank account dry can be embarrassing, costly, and time-consuming. The best way to avoid it is to keep track of your money, plan your spending, and be a smart shopper.

Credit Cards: Buy Now, Pay Later

Credit cards look the same as debit cards. Both are flat pieces of plastic you swipe or insert into a card reader. The biggest difference between a debit and credit card is how the money moves from you to the store. A debit card purchase transfers money directly from your bank account to the store.

A credit card purchase, on the other hand, is more like a loan. The credit card company pays for your purchase immediately, and you have a fixed, or predetermined, period of time to pay back the credit card company.

If you don't pay on time, the company charges late fees and a high rate of interest. And you end up owing more than the price of the items you purchased.

Convenience, but at a Price

Credit cards are convenient, particularly for online shopping, but they can be costly if you miss a scheduled payment or don't repay the entire amount of the balance on your card in full. You can't apply for your own credit card until you are 18 years old (19 in some Canadian provinces). Your parents or guardians are allowed to add you as an authorized user on their cards, though, when you are younger. It's up to your parents—and the rules of their credit card company—to decide when you're ready to have access to a credit card.

Certain credit card companies also offer debit cards. These work exactly like regular debit cards. When you pay with a VISA debit card, for example, money is transferred from your bank account to the store. The only difference is that this card is issued by a credit card company, while a regular debit card is issued by your financial institution.

Prepaid: Another Link to Your Stash

Prepaid cards became fashionable at the end of the 20th century. Gift cards for specific stores began to replace paper gift certificates in the 1980s. About 15 years later, prepaid credit cards came into being. Both types of cards are pre-loaded with a certain amount of money that the cardholder deposits into a special account connected to the card.

When you use the card, the cashier swipes it, and the amount you spend is deducted from the total available in the account. Say you have a $50 gift card for your favorite clothing store, and you buy a T-shirt for $30. That means you have $20 left on your card to use another time. Prepaid credit cards work the same way. Because you put money into the card account *before* you make a purchase, prepaid credit cards are not technically *credit* cards. But they look like ordinary credit cards and can be used at any business that accepts that type of credit card.

BE CAREFUL OUT THERE

PROTECT YOUR PIN

To use debit cards, and for some credit-card purchases or payments, you have to have a Personal Identification Number, or PIN. This is a secret code that identifies *you* as the owner of the card in question. When using a debit card at a store or ATM, you must punch your PIN into a machine before you can pay or withdraw money. That way, the machine knows you are authorized to use the card—and the money it connects to.

This is for your protection, to make sure nobody else can use your card to buy things or steal your money. Other than you, the only people who should know your PIN are your parents or guardians. Do not reveal your PIN to *anyone* else. This is one secret that's not for sharing.

iPad mini 2 32GB for
$49.99*

on a 2-year agreement with purchase of any iPhone

*Svc activation req'd on both devices.

Get yours today!

Call 888.123.4567
Customer Call-In Code: 24-8517-9795

Click XYZ.com/youripadmini2

Visit your XYZ store

Make switching

Only $49.99 for a new iPad? Sounds like a sweet deal! At least that's what the text you can read says. If you can make out the light-gray print on most of this advertisement, you'll see that you need to sign up for a two-year plan and buy a new iPhone. You may have a difficult time reading or understanding all of the text. Some ads purposely overburden and confuse the buyer with such complicated items as **taxes,** penalties for canceling services, fees for data, "bundling" of services, and more. Talk about fine print! Buyer beware!

PayPal: A Favorite Online Link to Cash

PayPal wasn't the world's first online payment system, but it was the first one to take hold in North America. This system is used for online purchases, and is considered more secure than using a credit card. Every time you use a credit card, you give out personal information such as your billing address, not to mention your credit card number, to the store or online site. When you use PayPal, however, you give out your information once to set up your account, then you shop at different stores or sites using this password-protected account. That way, you've only shared your information with PayPal, not every site you buy from. You have to be 18 years old to open a PayPal account.

The Fine Print

Planning your purchases, making informed shopping choices, and knowing how to pay are some of the keys to smart spending. Reading the fine print is another one.

You'd be surprised at how many hidden costs, rules, and commitments are involved in spending money.

Online shopping, for example, is convenient but often comes with hidden costs. These may include shipping charges and **currency-exchange** fees if, for instance, you're a Canadian shopping on a U.S. site. Make sure you know the *total* cost of an item before you buy it online. Read the return policy, too, to find out how much it will cost to send the item back if it's damaged, it isn't what you expected, or it doesn't fit.

$PEAKING OF MONEY ...

"95% or more of the time, cell phone insurance is not worth buying."

Logan Abbott, president of Wirefly, a website offering online comparisons of smartphones and cell phone plans

Cell Phones: Lots More Than Buying a Phone!

Cell phone plans are another place to watch for hidden-cost hazards. Taxes, charges for phone service outside the area of your local network (called roaming charges), and other unexpected fees can quickly double the advertised monthly price of a plan.

When you buy a cell phone or other electronic equipment, such as a laptop or tablet, always be prepared for the extended warranty pitch. An extended warranty is a form of insurance or

a guarantee. For an additional fee, paid for by the customer, a warranty usually covers the repair or replacement of the device if it is broken. These plans can be costly—as much as half the purchase price for small items. "Fine print" describes what *is* covered and, more importantly, what is *not*. Find out what are the most common problems with the item you're buying and how often it has been known to fail for other customers. Then, decide for yourself. Do you need the extra warranty? Or is it a way for the store to make more money?

These are just a few examples of hidden costs to be aware of. The goal is not to scare you out of spending money, but to set you on the road to becoming a confident consumer.

What Would You Do?

HOW BEST TO SNACK?

What do you do when you're hungry in the middle of the day? You might stop at a gas station and plunk down your cash for a bag of chips and a soda. Sometimes it's hard to resist that candy-bar rack on the way to the checkout!

Or are you someone who brings along a bottle of water, an apple, and some other snacks when you leave the house?

If you're like many people, you probably opt for the quick sugar rush from tasty junk food! But, as with most choices that involve spending money, there are **trade-offs**. Check out the chart below to get you thinking about spending and snacking.

JUNK FOOD	"HEALTHY" FOOD
Usually doesn't spoil; can eat anytime	Can spoil; may need to be replaced with another purchase
Empty **calories** won't fill you up for long; you'll have to buy more soon	Fill you up longer; you won't need to buy another snack soon
Can be bought almost anywhere	Less readily available at convenience stores
Packaging creates garbage that doesn't break down	Organic waste breaks down but you need to find an organics disposal bin
Sugar and chemicals can be bad for your teeth	Natural ingredients don't harm your teeth, and crispy fruit and veggies can even clean your teeth and make them stronger!
Expensive and usually a small portion	Can be cheaper, especially bought in bulk

Some of these trade-offs involve cost and convenience. Others are about making "smart" choices that might be less convenient, but could pay off in the long run.

See if you can add more trade-offs to this list by finding out more about what you eat when you snack. For example, you can use the snack's packaging or online resources to figure out some things about the ingredients in your snack. Was it high in calories? How do you think the trade-offs you discover will affect your buying and snacking decisions?

REALITY CHECKS

Everybody needs money to survive, but not everyone has enough. Some people struggle to make ends meet. They might have to rely on **charities** for their basic food, clothing, and healthcare needs. Not-for-profit charities, which may offer people services such as a safe bed to sleep in or food to eat, also require financial help to continue helping others because they do not make their own money. When money comes into your life, it's wise to save some and spend some—but you might also consider giving some of it away to help others.

Spend $ on Yourself!

Spend $ on Others!

Studies have shown that if people have extra money, they often feel better using it to help others than spending it on things for themselves.

Food
Donations

Give to Others and Invest in Yourself

You've probably heard the saying, "It's better to give than to receive." It turns out that's not just something your parents say to you to teach you a lesson about selflessness. Study after study shows that people who give money away are happier than those who don't. Helping others makes them feel good about themselves, and feel gratitude for what they have.

Recent studies have shown that giving to **charity** decreases stress levels and changes the donor's brain chemistry for the better. It lights up the parts of the brain related to pleasure, social connection, and trust.

If you are in a position to give, why not conduct your own research? Check out the charities in your area that are helping others. Try donating to a cause you care about and see how it makes you feel!

F⊙CUS ON FINANCE

Charity Can Be Heart-Healthy for You!

Studies have shown that giving to others can have a positive emotional effect on those who give. But can generosity also help your physical health? In a 2015 Canadian study, psychologist Elizabeth Dunn did research on how having money affected people's emotional and physical well-being. One of her findings was that donating to charity lowers a person's **blood pressure**. Giving is "not just heartwarming," she said. "It may be quite literally good for our hearts."

37

Make Giving One of Your Goals

If you decide to donate regularly, plan for this sum in your budget. Right now, if you've already started sorting your money into three pots—emergency money, financial-goal money, and spending money—donations will probably come out of the spending money segment. On the other hand, if you'd like to make a large donation to a particular organization in the future, you could add that to your list of longer-term goals and save up your donation dollars.

Not everyone is in a position to donate dollars, but there are other ways to contribute to causes you care about. Volunteering your time and giving goods, such as food or clothing, are equally valuable and generous acts.

Lessons Learned

In this book, you've learned the importance of making plans for your money. You found out that banks and credit unions are safe places for saving. You now know the value of thinking before you spend your hard-earned bucks, and the benefits of donating your dollars to charity.

Another important thing to know is that most governments have consumer protection laws and practices to safeguard you and your money when it comes to saving and spending. These laws are designed to prevent **fraud** and unethical, or dishonest, practices by businesses. They also make sure individuals have access to a variety of fair, safe, and reliable products and services.

Volunteers from the U.S. Navy serve food to poor and homeless people in a soup kitchen in Salinas, California. Giving your time and energy to helping others is as valuable as donating money to charity.

BE CAREFUL OUT THERE

THE OPPOSITE OF CHARITY

Always involve an adult when you are considering donating goods, time, or dollars to charity. Sadly, money makes greedy people do dishonest things. Some even pretend to operate charities so they can steal money from kind people. Often, they operate on online fundraising sites to raise donations for a false cause. For example, a common scam involves a rip-off artist faking a life-threatening illness to convince people to send them money.

Do your research before handing out your hard-earned dollars to any charity. Whether it's a request for money on the phone, through the mail, in an email, or at your front door, make sure the organization is real, that it does what it promises to do, and that your money goes directly to the people, animals, or groups that need it.

CHOOSE A CHARITY

If you decide to donate money, countless organizations would love to have it. Who do you want to help? Here are some things you can do to help you decide:

1. Based on the financial planning you've done, figure out how much money you can afford to donate. Decide if you will make a donation each month, once a year, or one time only.

2. Make a list of causes you care about. Your list might include environmental issues, education, animal rescue, disaster relief, or safety for women and children.

3. Research charities in each of these categories. Most charities have websites where you can find information. Be sure to ask a trusted adult to help you search online and watch out for online scams. What does the charity do? How can you help? What percentage of the charity's income goes directly to programs or people, versus **overhead costs**? Where will your support do the most good, or where are the charity's areas of need?

4. Based on your research, make a short list of charities you would like to support. Discuss each of them with your parents or guardians to help you decide which one(s) you might get involved with.

5. If it's possible, visit the offices of the charities in question or talk with a representative of each charity. Do this with a trusted adult. Ask questions and learn more to help make your decision.

6. Choose a charity or two to help. Decide whether you will donate money or donate your time.

There are also consumer protection organizations that help find justice for people who believe they've been ripped off. They also aim to prevent false advertising–untrue, confusing, or misleading information used to sell a product or service.

Your parents, guardians, and other trusted adults in your life are also there to help you with important financial decisions. This all means that, when it comes to saving and spending, you're not alone!

SPEND

FUTURE

EDUCATION

FUN

BE CAREFUL OUT THERE

MONEY BETWEEN FRIENDS

Another way to use your money to help others is to loan it out. This can be dangerous, though. Many friendships have been lost over borrowed money that's not paid back. There's nothing wrong with helping out a buddy with the loan of a fiver now and then. If your buddy doesn't pay you back, though, think twice before you offer them money again.

Whenever you lend money, to anyone, make sure you have a clear agreement about when that money is to be repaid. Keep clear records to track the loan and payback schedule. Talk to an adult if someone–even your best friend–asks to borrow a large amount of money. You could choose to give them a loan, but you might think about writing a contract, or written agreement, to hold them to a repayment schedule.

SAVE

CHARITIES

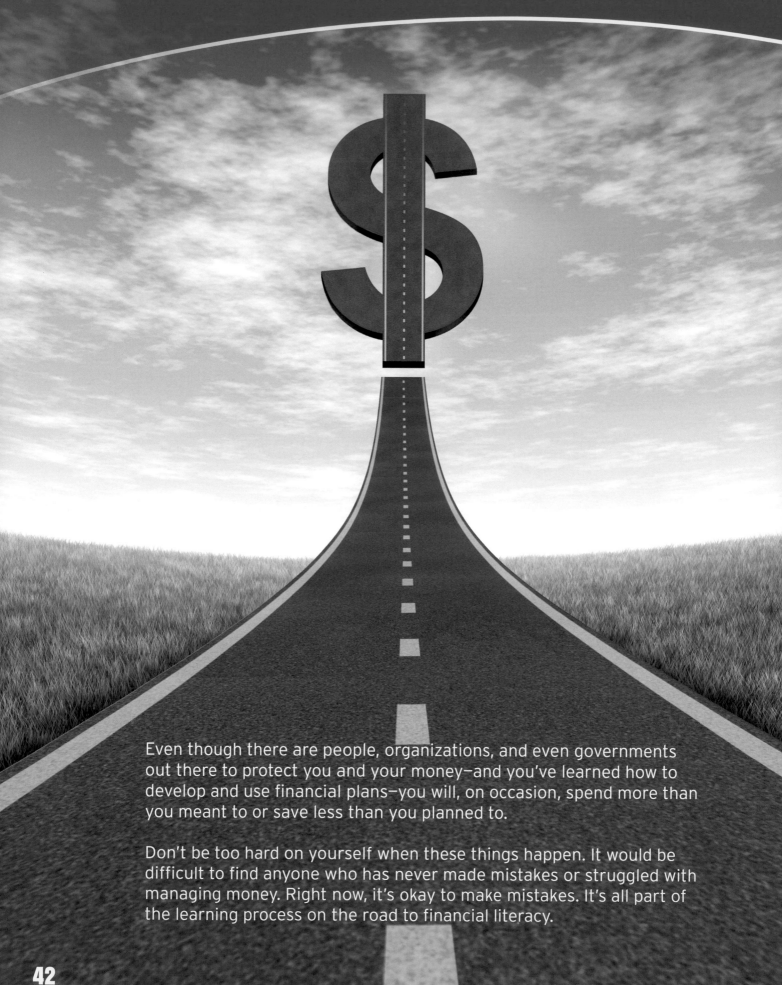

Even though there are people, organizations, and even governments out there to protect you and your money—and you've learned how to develop and use financial plans—you will, on occasion, spend more than you meant to or save less than you planned to.

Don't be too hard on yourself when these things happen. It would be difficult to find anyone who has never made mistakes or struggled with managing money. Right now, it's okay to make mistakes. It's all part of the learning process on the road to financial literacy.

DON'T BELIEVE EVERYTHING YOU READ-OR SEE

As you go through life, you will be bombarded by advertising. No matter how appealing, entertaining, or emotionally powerful an advertisement might be, its main goal is to sell you something. Ads often show happy people using a product. The message is that you, too, will be happy if you buy and use that product.

Beware the word "new" in advertising. The goal of this message is to convince you that the products you currently have are outdated and no longer popular—even if they still work well. Some businesses disguise ads as information, or use **statistics** to prove their product is preferable. The "**cola wars**" are the most famous example of this. In the 1980s, Coke and Pepsi each used sales statistics to prove their soda was the best you could buy. How was that possible? Each used different statistics—each soda was number one in a different sales category. In this way, both companies tricked customers into believing they were at the top of the list.

Today, the cola wars have evolved into advertising that we know as infomercials. Often showing up as "paid programming" in your TV listings, these half- and full-hour programs have the appearance of newscasts or talk shows. In reality, they are ads for things ranging from household appliances to clothes, jewelry, and health- and beauty-enhancing products.

It's important to understand advertising for what it is—a way to sway your spending. Bottom line: Question everything you read, see, and hear when it comes to handing over your money.

GLOSSARY

accountable Bearing or accepting responsibility for something

app Short for "application"; a program or piece of software, as on a computer, smartphone, or tablet, designed to perform a particular task or service for the user

automatic payment A regular payment that a customer with a bank account authorizes the bank to pay another person or business; the money for the payment is withdrawn from the customer's account

barter To exchange, or trade, goods and services for other goods and services

bookkeeping Keeping records of a person or business's finances

boutique A small store, or a small shop within a larger department store, that sells fashionable clothes, jewelry, or other items; often the word "boutique" is used to describe any store that sells highly specialized goods or services, usually at higher prices

blood pressure The pressure in your blood vessels, measured by two numbers, when your heart beats and when it rests between beats

branch (of a bank) A location of a bank, other than the main office, where a customer can do business in person

budget (noun) An estimate of how much money comes in and goes out of a household or business in a given period of time; the amount of money needed or available for a purpose, such as running a household

calories A unit of heat energy; sometimes measured by the amount of food that produces one calorie of energy

check A written order directing a bank to pay money from a customer's account

charity A group that helps people in need

child's play A task that is easily done

cola wars A series of advertising campaigns launched by rival soft drink producers Coke and Pepsi, to encourage individuals to choose their respective products

corporation A large business organization or a collection of business organizations

credit card A card with which a person can buy things and pay for them later

currency exchange A marketplace where a person can buy or sell money from different countries

debit card A bank-issued card that allows the holder to withdraw money, or pay for something, directly from his or her bank account

financial institution A business whose primary purpose is to deal with money; banks and credit unions are financial institutions

fraud Using dishonest methods to take something valuable from another person

impulse A sudden urge to act or do something that wasn't planned

impulse buy A spur-of-the-moment purchase made without thinking

income Money earned or otherwise acquired

insurance Financial protection, paid for in advance, in case something goes wrong in areas such as health, disability, or auto, home, and business ownership; customers pay regular fees to an insurance company, which covers customers' costs when the need arises

interest A fee paid to borrow someone else's money

interest rate A portion of an amount owed, usually expressed as a percentage, that determines how much interest is added to the original amount

invest To purchase something now to make money in the future

long-term financial goal Something a person wants to do or buy in the future

medium-term financial goal Something a person wants to do or buy soon but not right away

minimum balance The least amount of money a person is required to keep in a bank account

not-for-profit (or nonprofit) organization An organization that doesn't earn extra money; all the money it makes goes back into the business

online banking A way to manage your money and bank accounts on the Internet, rather than in person

overdraft A shortage in a bank account caused by withdrawing more money than the account has in it; the term "overdraft" or "overdraft protection" may also refer to a set amount of money the bank permits a customer to overdraw from his or her account, usually for a fee

overdraw To withdraw more money from a bank account than has been deposited into the account

overhead costs Ongoing expenses involved in operating a business that aren't directly related to the business's money-making activities; rent and electricity bills, for example, are overhead costs

PayPal An online payment system that allows buyers and sellers to transfer funds electronically, without use of money or checks

percent Parts per 100; often shown with the "%" sign, which stands for "percent"; if 40 percent of all kids take buses to school, that means "40 out of 100"; this number describes the ratio, number, or rate of kids taking buses out of a larger group

point of sale The place where you pay for something—for example, a cashier's counter at a store

priority Something that is treated as more important than other things

profit Financial gain; money earned by a company or person, after paying the costs of running the business

remorse Regret for having done something

secure Safe from danger

short list A small number of candidates selected from a larger group; finalists in a competition, for example

short-term financial goal Something a person wants to do or buy very soon

stakes Things that can be gained or lost by taking a risk

statistics Facts usually based on a study of a large amount of numerical information

status Social or professional rank

strategy A plan for, or approach to, something

taboo Forbidden; prohibited or restricted by social custom

tax A fee charged by the government to individuals and businesses based such factors as income (income tax), the cost of certain items (sales tax), or the value of a house or other real estate (property tax); these charges are used to support the operation of the government and to help pay for services provided by the government

therapeutic Having a positive effect on the body or mind; helping create a sense of being comfortable or happy

trade-off A balance between two features that are both appealing but don't necessarily go together

withdraw To remove or take away

FURTHER INFORMATION

BOOKS

Butler, Tamsen. *The Complete Guide to Personal Finance: For Teenagers and College Students* (revised second edition). Atlantic Publishing Group, Inc., 2010.

Dakers, Diane. *The Bottom Line: Money Basics* (Financial Literacy for Life). Crabtree Publishing, 2017.

It Doesn't Grow on Trees: Sources of Income (Financial Literacy for Life). Crabtree Publishing, 2017.

Holyoke, Nancy. *Money: How to Make It, Save It, and Spend It* (A Smart Girl's Guide). American Girl Publishing, 2014.

McGuire, Kara. *Smart Spending: The Teens' Guide to Cash, Credit, and Life's Costs*. Compass Point Books, 2015.

WEBSITES

www.themint.org/
The Mint is a website designed to teach financial literacy skills to kids, teens, parents, and teachers. It includes information, games, and tools to help you learn.

http://read.marvel.com/#/labelbook/41238
This link takes you to a free graphic novel, *Guardians of the Galaxy: Rocket's Powerful Plan*. In this book, Ant-Man, Hulk, Black Widow, and others join the Guardians in a money-saving adventure.

www.moneyandyouth.cfee.org/en/
This website, called *Money and Youth: A Guide to Financial Literacy*, is for kids and grown-ups who want to learn about finances. It includes a full glossary, links to other sites, and an excellent Q&A section. It also offers a link to a free, and excellent, e-book.

www.pbskids.org/itsmylife/money/index.html
It's My Life: Money is an informative site created by PBS Kids. It is divided into several sections, including games, a special feature on a subject of interest to kids, such as babysitting, and three major topics—Making Money, Spending Smarts, and Managing Money. Each topic includes information, discussions, and tools to help you learn about your money.

http://moneytalks4teens.ucanr.edu/
Created by the University of California, *Money Talks (Cuida Tu Dinero)*, is a bilingual website designed to teach young people about financial management. It offers excellent tips, surveys, info, and tools. Unfortunately, some of the links listed are out of date. Otherwise, it is an excellent resource.

INDEX

ABOUT THE AUTHOR

Diane Dakers was born and raised in Toronto, and now makes her home in Victoria, British Columbia. She has written three fiction and 18 nonfiction books for young people. Diane is dedicated to personal financial planning. She saves for the future, regularly donates to charity, and considers herself a super-shopper. Thanks to coupons, sales, and store reward points, Diane rarely pays full price for anything!